Walk Around

MW00581803

By LCDR Richard S. Dann, USNR
Color by Don Greer

F6F Hellcat

Walk Around Number 9

squadron/signal publications

Introduction

In writing this book, my second in the Walk Around series, I have developed an appreciation for the aircraft that has defined the role of modern carrier aircraft. During my first fourteen weeks in the Navy (at Aviation Officer Candidate School), it was drilled into our heads that naval aviation was "fleet protection and power projection." True, this is the role of the modern carrier battle group, but it was the Hellcat that was the first carrier "strike fighter." Not only was it adequate in dealing with the Japanese air threat, it was also able to destroy both the Japanese infrastructure and the morale of her military in the air-to-ground role. It performed both "fleet protection' and "power projection" equally well. In fact, toward the end of the Second World War, the numbers of torpedo bombers and dive bombers aboard carriers were reduced to make room for more Hellcats (VBF squadrons). This measure was taken primarily in response to the Kamikaze threat, but also left the option open to go on the offensive. This alone underscores the significance of the Hellcat in the Pacific War.

Below is a list of restored Hellcats used in the production of this book and present location:

Model	BuNo	Location
F6F-3	41930	McLellan-Palomar Airport, Carlsbad, California
F6F-3	42874	San Diego Aerospace Museum, San Diego, California
F6F-3	66237	National Museum of Naval Aviation, Pensacola, Florida
F6F-5	79192	New England Air Museum, Windsor Locks, CT.
F6F-5	93897	Planes of Fame, Chino, California

I would like to thank two people for their efforts in helping me complete this book. First, Mr. Roger Seybel, a volunteer at the Grumman History Center and Mr Larry Webster, whose rebuilt F6F-5 BuNo 79192 have set the standard for all future Hellcat restorations.

Acknowledgements:

Mark Aldrich	Hill Goodspeed	John Fry
Carl Snow	Sid Bradd	Jan Jacobs
Richard & Doris Hargis	Lieutenant Ken Acosta	Dick Martin
Richard M. Hill	HOPS! Bistro and Brewery	Jack Kelly
Cheyenne Gringeri-Brown	Cinema Air Jet Center	Ray Wagner
Eddie Valenzuela	Northrop-Grumman	Tailhook Association
San Diego Aerospace Museum	Captain Richard "Zeke" Cormier, USN, Ret.	
Colonel R. Bruce Porter USMC, Ret.	Tom Phillips	Janet Ryan
Tony Bunch	August Heiss	Jerry Foster

ISBN 0-89747-079-6

If you have any photographs of aircraft, armor, soldiers or ships of any nation, particularly wartime snapshots, why not share them with us and help make Squadron/Signal's books all the more interesting and complete in the future. Any photograph sent to us will be copied and the original returned. The donor will be fully credited for any photos used. Please send them to:

Squadron/Signal Publications, Inc.
1115 Crowley Drive
Carrollton, TX 75011-5010

Если у вас есть фотографии самолётов, вооружения, солдат или кораблей любой страны, особенно, снимки времён войны, поделитесь с нами и помогите сделать новые книги издательства Эскадрон/Сигнал ещё интереснее. Мы переснимем ваши фотографии и вернём оригиналы. Имена приславших снимки будут сопровождать все опубликованные фотографии. Пожалуйста, присылайте фотографии по адресу:

Squadron/Signal Publications, Inc.
1115 Crowley Drive
Carrollton, TX 75011-5010

軍用機、装甲車両、兵士、軍艦などの写真を所持しておられる方はいらっしゃいませんか？どの国のものでも結構です。作戦中に撮影されたものが特に良いのです。Squadron/Signal社の出版する刊行物において、このような写真は内容を一層充実し、興味深くすることができます。当方にお送り頂いた写真は、複写の後お返しいたします。出版物中に写真を使用した場合は、必ず提供者のお名前を明記させて頂きます。お写真は下記にご送付ください。

Squadron/Signal Publications, Inc.
1115 Crowley Drive
Carrollton, TX 75011-5010

A F6F-5 of VF-82 awaits its turn to launch from USS BENNINGTON (CV-20). The catapult bridle is visible ahead of the belly tank. Although difficult to see, the catapult holdback is attached to the extreme rear of the fuselage. When launch tension is reached, a fitting on the holdback would fail, allowing the aircraft to takeoff. (Tailhook)

Overleaf: A F6F-5N of Night Development Squadron Two (VCN-2). The aircraft is armed with 20MM cannon inboard with extended barrels and flash suppressors. The landing gear doors and radome are painted White. The national insignia wraps over the rear portion of the radome fairing. (Tailhook)

This F6F-3 of VF-11 illustrates the primary identification features of the F6F-3 including the early style windshield, lower cowling flaps (BuNos 04775-04958, 08798-09047 and 25721-26195). The small exhaust fairing was also found on these aircraft as well as BuNos 39999-40235, after which it was deleted. (Tailhook)

The configurations of the ailerons was another identification of the F6F-3. The -3 had a controllable trim tab on the port aileron and a fixed tab on the starboard aileron. This F6F-3 was assigned to VF-44. (Tailhook)

Grumman F6F-3 Hellcat

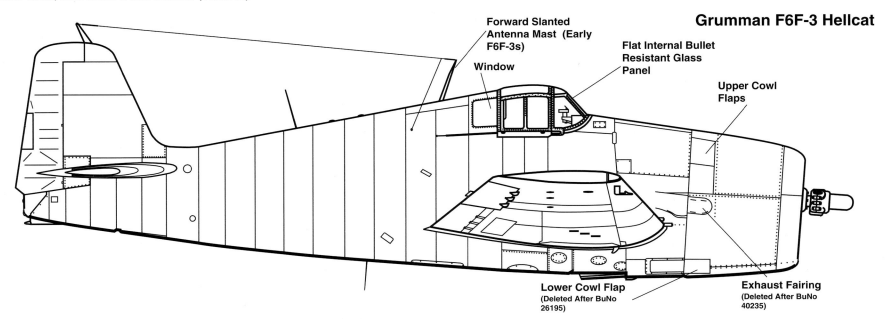

Forward Slanted Antenna Mast (Early F6F-3s)

Window

Flat Internal Bullet Resistant Glass Panel

Upper Cowl Flaps

Lower Cowl Flap
(Deleted After BuNo 26195)

Exhaust Fairing
(Deleted After BuNo 40235)

Belching smoke from its exhausts, an early production F6F-3 starts its Pratt & Whitney engine. The cowl flaps, intercooler doors,and oil cooler are all in the open position. It appears that this Hellcat was previously painted with the national insignia in six positions and has the port underwing position painted out. 4,403 F6F-3s were built from September of 1942 until April of 1944, at which time production shifted to the improved F6F-5 Hellcat. The aircraft number was painted in three positions on the cowling and on the upper landing gear doors. (Tailhook)

4

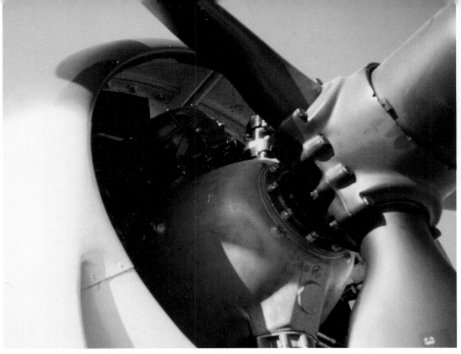

The Pratt & Whitney R-2800 engine is equipped with two magnetos for ignition mounted at the top of the forward crankcase. The propeller governor is at the top of the crankcase between the magnetos. (Author)

The F6F-3 was equipped with a Hamilton Standard three blade constant speed propeller that was thirteen feet one inch in diameter. Oil pressure was used to adjust the blade pitch via the propeller governor. (Author)

This late production F6F-3 (BuNo 41930) has two upper cowl flaps and no lower cowl flap. The engine was designed as a Quick Engine Change (QEC) unit, which was received from the factory complete with mount, oil tank, cowling, exhaust and ignition systems in place for quick installations. (Author)

5

F6F Bureau Number Breakdown

BuNo. (F6F-3)	Fabrication Sequence	Delivery Dates	Notes
04775-04958	1-184	09/42-04/43	Includes 20 to U.K. (FN320-FN339)
08798-09047	185-434	04/43-06/43	Includes 30 to U.K. (FN340-FN369)
25721-26195	435-909	06/43-08/43	Includes 50 to U.K. (FN370-FN419)
65890-66244	910-1264	07/43-09/43	Includes 30 to U.K. (FN420-FN449)
			Includes 24 F6F-3N
			BuNo 66244 built as XF6F-2, later rebuilt as last F6F-3.
39999-43137	1265-4403	09/43-04/44	Includes 122 to U.K (JV100-JV189, JV190-JV221)
			Includes 205 F6F-3N, 18 F6F-3E.

BuNo (F6F-5)			
58000-58999	4404-5403	04/44-0644	Includes 80 to U.K. (JV222-JV301), includes 107 F6F-5N
69992-72991	5404-8403	06/44-12/44	Includes 446 to U.K. (JV302-JV324, JW700-JW784, JW857-JW889, JX670-JX964), 3 F6F-3Ns (JX965-JX967).
			Includes 434 F6F-5Ns
77259-80258	8404-11403	12/44-06/45	Includes 292 F6F-5 and 77 F6F-5Ns to U.K, (JX968-JX999, KD108-KD160, KE118-KE233, plus 5 unknowns.)
93652-94521	11404-12273	06/45-11/45	Includes 32 to U.K. (KE234-KE265).
			Includes 369 F6F-5Ns.

Production Totals

	To USN	To U.K.
F6F-3	3904	252
F6F-3N	229	
F6F-3E	18	
F6F-5	5584	850
F6F-5N	1354	80
XF6F-6	2	
	11,091	1182

Total: 12,273

Note: These tables were compiled by the late Richard M. Hill

(Right) This F6F-5 (BuNo 78855) was the 10,000 Hellcat built and was delivered to the Navy on 14 March 1945. 78855 served in combat aboard the USS TICONDEROGA during the closing days of the Second World War. (Grumman)

This Hellcat was the prototype F6F-5 (BuNo 25881). The aircraft had a F6F-5 style windshield, but an unusual canopy. The canopy was a single piece blown Plexiglas bubble type. This was the only Hellcat to ever carry this type of canopy, but engineering drawings at Grumman indicate that this canopy arrangement was considered for production. (Grumman)

The power plant on the F6F-3 was the Pratt & Whitney R-2800-10 radial, which had a two stage, two speed supercharger and developed over 2,000 hp. The outer intakes fed the superchargers and the two supercharger intercooler doors are in the open position. The center intake fed the oil cooler. (Author)

F6F-3 (BuNo 41930) has the engine cowl flaps in the full open position. The technique of building airframes from flat aluminum sheets on the fuselage sped up production of the Hellcat tremendously and made for an extremely strong structure. In just over three years, 12,275 F6Fs were produced. (Author)

New production F6F-3 line the Grumman Bethpage ramp awaiting delivery. The camouflage scheme was Non-specular Sea Blue, Non-specular Intermediate Blue over Inisignia White undersurfaces. All aircraft are fitted with the standard 150 gallon Hellcat underfuselage centerline external fuel tank. Hellcats were built exclusively by Grumman, unlike the Wildcat and Avenger, which were also built by the Eastern Aircraft Division of General Motors. (Tailhook)

This F6F-3 of VF-5 flipped over during a landing accident. The lower cowling flaps indicate that this was an early production F6F-3. The arresting hook is in the fully extended position. A number of features are visible, including the three shell ejection chutes in each wing, the starboard underwing bomb rack, wheel wells, ventral recognition lights, flap and aileron hinge lines and wing fold panels. The starboard elevator is a different color from the rest of the underside, indicating that it was probably a replacement part. (Tailhook)

Navy Ace, Lieutenant (Junior Grade) Alex Vraciu on the wing of his F6F-3 of VF-6. The catapult bridle hooks are visible just inboard of the landing gear doors. The cowl flaps and intercooler doors are open and the starboard bomb rack is visible along with its sway braces. LTJG Vraciu finished the war with a total of nineteen kills. (USN via R. M. Hill)

A F6F-3 (BuNo 04778) on the grass at the Grumman Bethpage facility. Very early production F6F-3 had oversized main landing gear doors like those used on the prototype. This aircraft also has smooth tires and an inflatable tailwheel. The landing light is also visible under the port wing. This feature was deleted on the 273rd Hellcat. Night fighter variants, however, retained the light. (USMC via Tailhook)

A pair of flight deck crewmen prepare to pull chocks on an early F6F-3. Only the first 909 F6F-3 (BuNos 04775-26195) had the forward canted radio mast on the fuselage spine and inboard machine gun fairing. The outboard gun ports are taped over. (Tailhook via R. M. Hill)

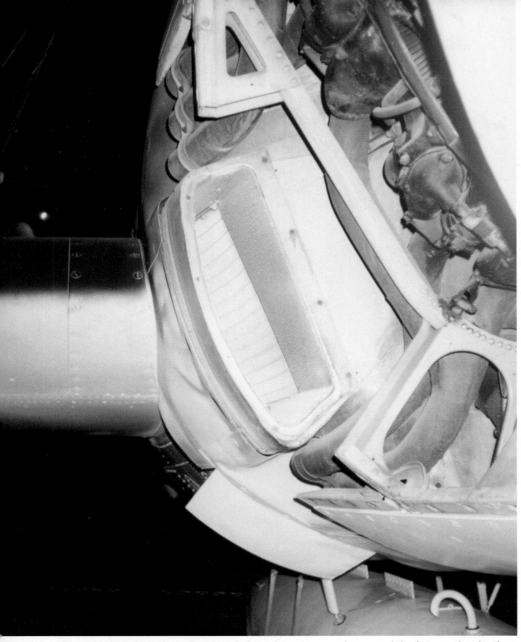

There are three exhaust stacks exiting on the upper side of the engine and two lower on the fuselage. The cowling was held in place by Dzus fasteners. Below the engine cylinders is the duct that supplies cooling air to the oil cooler and air to the auxiliary stage supercharger. (Author)

The Yellow (non-standard) tank visible above the engine mount is the aircraft's oil tank. Supercharged combustion air entered the carburetor through the large Zinc Chromate Green ducts. The carburetor is visible just forward of the oil tank. (Author)

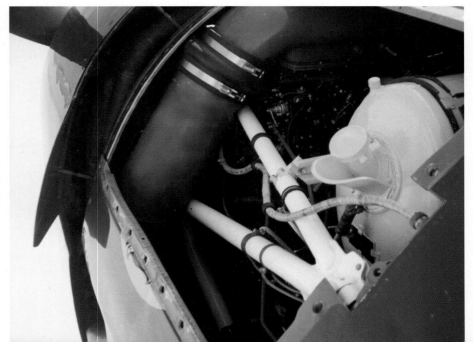

The lower starboard cowling panels have been removed to reveal the intercooler ducting. The intercooler cooled the superheated compressed air coming from the supercharger prior to entry into the carburetor. This reduced the chance of detonation and preignition. Also visible are the sway braces and banding straps that held the external Mk XII fuel tank in place. (Author)

F6F Exhaust Stack Arrangement

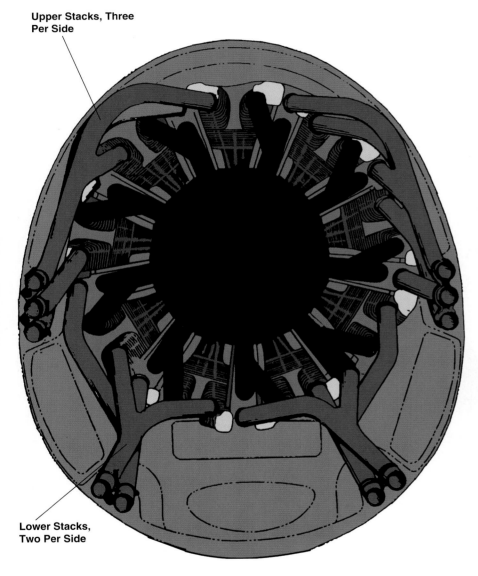

Upper Stacks, Three Per Side

Lower Stacks, Two Per Side

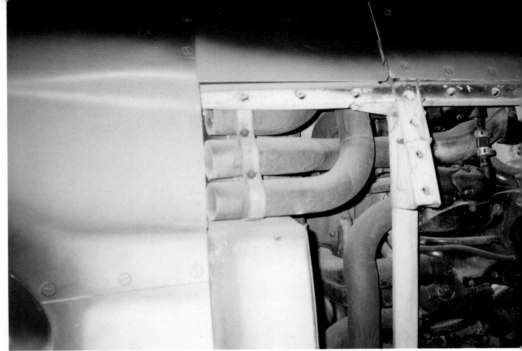

The upper set of exhaust stacks on a F6F-3. The upper stacks collected gasses from five cylinders (per side), while the lower stacks collected gasses from four cylinders per side. (Author)

The lower set of exhausts stacks on a F6F-3. The intercooler shutter is directly behind the lower exhaust port. Also visible is part of the oil cooler/supercharger ducting. (Author)

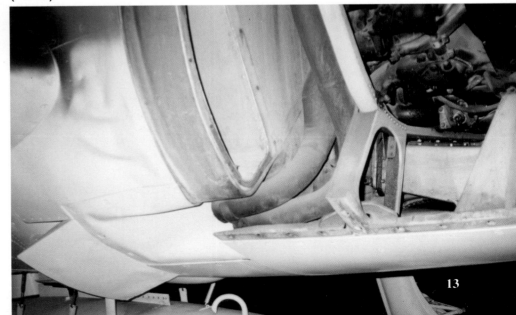

13

The port main wheel of the San Diego Aerospace Museum's F6F-3 Hellcat. The Hellcat was equipped with disc brakes. Visible just behind the wheel is a portion of the under fuselage 150 gallon external fuel tank. (Author)

The starboard main landing gear of San Diego's F6F-3 (BuNo 42874). This restored Hellcat is fitted with original eight spoke Hellcat wheels, while most flyable restorations are fitted with a variety of wheel types, probably due to the rarity of original Hellcat wheels. (Author)

The tailwheel of the San Diego Aerospace Museum F6F-3 (BuNo 42874). Hellcats were equipped with a full-swivel hard rubber tailwheel that was ten and a half inches in diameter and four inches wide. There are at least three surviving F6F-3s, one at the National Museum of Naval Aviation, one at San Diego and a flyable example at Palomar Airport in Carlsbad, California. (Author)

During retraction the main landing gear of the F6F rotates ninety degrees to lay flat in the landing gear well. The oleo strut is at its full extension and the torque arms are also fully extended. (Grumman)

The landing gear in the fully retracted position. The outline of all three landing gear doors is visible as is the outline of the wing fold drop panel. The catapult attachment fitting doubles as a jack point for the Hellcat. (Grumman)

The inboard landing gear well with the wing in the folded position. The hook in the center is the landing gear up lock, which swings outward and up to lock the landing gear in place in the wheel well when the gear is in the retracted position. (Author)

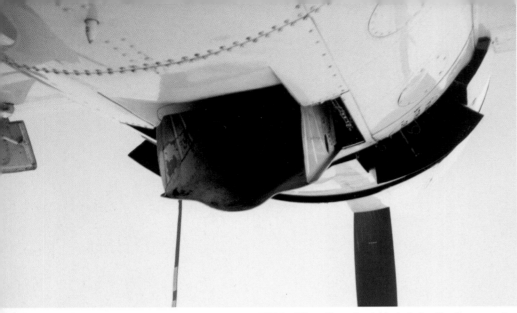

This is the oil cooler waste gate on a F6F-3. The oil cooler is fed air by the large center air intake in the front of the cowling. This same intake also supplies air to the auxiliary stage supercharger. The oil cooler gate is hydraulically actuated by a control located on the port side cockpit console. (Author)

Just above the open oil cooler waste gate is the fuel strainer drain access panel and several other circular inspection panels. There are several small drain ports also visible behind the waste gate on the lower fuselage. The lettering on the strainer drain is non-standard. (Author)

The open starboard intercooler flap in the fully open position. Just behind it is the fuel strainer drain access panel and forward of it is the lower exhaust port. The intercooler cooled air from the supercharger to the carburetor, lowering the risk of detonation or preignition. Later Hellcats (after the 1,900th F6F-3, BuNO 40634) had Anti-Detonant Injection (water/alcohol) which allowed for higher manifold pressures . (Author)

The main fuel and reserve fuel tank filler panels are located on the fuselage above the wing root. Forward of these is the hydraulic accumulator access panel. The hydraulic tank access panel is located just behind the unit marking. (Author)

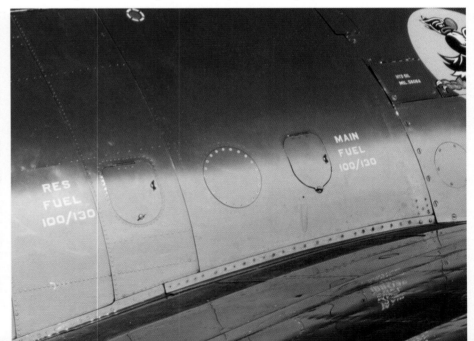

The landing gear on the F6F-3 was hydraulically operated from an engine driven hydraulic pump and rotated ninety degrees to lay flat within the wing. The landing gear control handle was located on the left side of the instrument panel. In case the hydraulic pump fails, the gear can be lowered by a hydraulic hand pump located on the right side of the seat. In the event of an total hydraulic failure the gear can be lowered by a nitrogen bottle , once. (Author)

The F6F-3 uses thirty-two by eight inch Goodyear tires and multiple disk brakes. The brakes had an independent hydraulic system with a master cylinder attached to each rudder pedal. Braking action was started by pressing down on the top of the rudder pedals. Tire inflation pressure differed, depending on aircraft gross weight and whether the aircraft was shore based or carrier based. (Author)

The F6F was considerably larger than the Wildcat, taking up sixteen feet two inches with the wings folded. The wide track landing gear made ground movements much easier than with the narrow track Wildcat. Although the F6F was able to be used on escort and light carriers (CVE/CVL), the FM-2 Wildcat was preferred because of the fact that more of them could be carried. (Author)

The F6F-3 Hellcat carried six .50 caliber machine guns with 400 rounds per gun. The barrels of the inboard guns extended beyond the wing leading edge, while the outboard gun was flush with the wing leading edge. The wing fold drop panels are also visible. The gun tubes on service aircraft were Black. (Author)

There are three spent shell casing ejector chutes beneath each wing on the F6F-3 Hellcat. The ejector chutes are staggered, as are the guns they serve. Inboard of each chute is the ammunition link ejector chute. The ammunition links are what hold the cartridges together forming an ammunition belt. Also visible are four of the flap hinges and the barrels for the .50 caliber machine guns. (Author)

The starboard wing root of a F6F-3 (BuNo 41930). The interior of the wing root was painted Zinc Chromate, however, the author has seen photographic evidence of aircraft with the wheel wells and wing roots painted in the same color as the aircraft underside, as well as other combinations. (Author)

The port wing root of BuNo 41930. The rear portion of the outer wing panel makes up the outer wall of the wheel well. The small hole in the leading edge of the wing is a cabin fresh air intake. A Type N-4 gun camera was also installed in the wing leading edge of port wing (although none has been installed in this restored aircraft). (Author)

The main landing gear wheels are single piece aluminum castings. The wheel brake flex line is visible behind the top portion of the landing gear strut. The landing gear door was three parts; one fixed to the landing gear strut, a smaller strut mounted door and a smaller section attached to the wing. These are late F6F-5 wheels, which were also used on B-52 outriggers. (Author)

The port main landing gear and gear doors. In the center of the lower main gear door is an oval inspection and strut servicing panel. The V shaped objects visible behind the wheel are the torque links. This aircraft has the recommended tire pressure stenciled on the gear door to aid in servicing the aircraft. (Author)

The main landing gear well of the F6F-3. The landing gear rotated ninety degrees to lay flat within the well. Also visible is the fully lowered inboard flap with its two circular inspection plates.

The interior of the starboard wheel well has a number of small hydraulic lines running through the lower corner. The red hook is the landing gear up lock that secured the landing gear into the well. Zinc Chromate Green was a non-standard color for Hellcat wheel wells, normally the well was painted in the same color as the surrounding exterior. (Author)

The landing gear was anchored to the main spar in the stub wing. With the wing in the folded position, the well was open on the outboard side. The small hook next to the landing gear is the catapult bridle hookup/jackpoint. (Author)

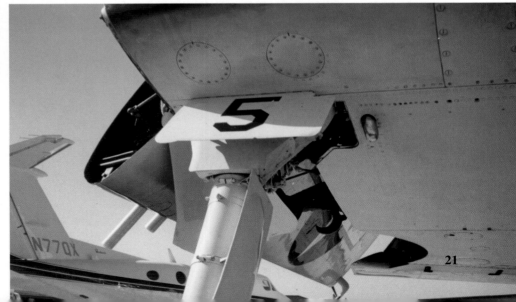

The small device just forward of the outer wing panel electrical quick disconnect junction box is a hydraulic wing lock timing switch. Barely visible under the electrical lines are the outer wing flap hydraulic lines. The small intake in the wing leading edge is the cabin fresh air inlet. (Author)

The object protruding upward from the wing surface is a Red (Orange on service aircraft) warning cylinder used to tell the pilot that the wings were not locked in the spread position. When locked, the cylinder would be flush with the wing surface. (Author)

The port wing root of a F6F-3 (BuNo 41930). Inside the wing fold is the wing electrical quick disconnect junction box (near the leading edge), wing fold pivot hinge, and wing fold actuating arm. The rods passing through the wing fold are the aileron tab connecting rod (upper) and aileron control connecting rod (lower). (Author)

The port wing in the retracted position. The aileron hinges are visible as are the flap closure doors just forward of the retracted flap. A piano hinge runs the length of the flap closure door. (Author)

The flaps on the F6F-3 are hydraulically actuated via the engine driven hydraulic pump. By use of a manual selector valve, the flaps can still be operated after an electrical failure. They can also be lowered by use of a hydraulic hand pump. It takes some thirty-five cycles of the hand pump to extend the flaps and twenty-five to retract them. (Author)

The starboard wing flaps of a F6F-3 in the full down position. The outboard flap section is fabric covered and is attached to the wing with three lever arms. The flap closure doors are visible. These are hinged sections that attach to the wing just forward of the flap and move upward to seal the gap left by the flaps as they are extended. (Author)

The starboard elevator and stabilizer of F6F-3 BuNo 41930. Both elevators are equipped with controllable trim tabs. The right and left elevator are interchangeable. Visible under the tail is the tail wheel tow bar used to move the aircraft. (Author)

The elevator trim tab was controlled by the pilot via a trim wheel in the cockpit. The tow bar was attached to the tail wheel by a through-bolt. Hellcats were towed backward via the tail wheel tow bar. (Author)

The vertical fin and rudder of F6F-3 BuNo 41930. Construction techniques for the Hellcat were similar to those used on the Wildcat. There were over 12,000 Hellcats built in just three years. Also visible is the elevator trim tab. Service F6F-3s were painted in non-specular (flat) colors. (Author)

The tail wheel of the F6F used a solid rubber tire for operations from carrier decks. When the aircraft was shore based, the solid tire was replaced with a pneumatic tire. The tail wheel was fully swiveling and could be locked in position for takeoff and landings. The wheel was raised and lowered hydraulically. (Author)

There are several inspection plates on the lower rear fuselage below the rudder. The tail hook retracts into a space under the rudder. (Author)

The extreme tail of the Hellcat housed the fully retractable arresting hook. The hook retracted into a space in the fuselage under the rudder. Just above the hook was a White position light. There is also a tie down/holdback fitting below the tail hook. (Author)

The pitot tube on the F6F was located under the starboard wingtip, near the wingtip position light. Like the earlier F4F Wildcat, the F6F had manually operated wing fold mechanisms. When delivered from the factory, the pitot tube was painted Red. (Author)

The star insignia on the underside of the wing was forty-five inches in diameter, with the Insignia Blue field being 50.62 inches in diameter. The position light on the starboard wing was Green, while the light on the port wing was Red. The aileron was fabric covered and had three hinges. (Author)

The top of the wing on the F6F held the gun bay access panels which were hinged at the leading edge. They were secured with Dzus fasteners. In the open position, the forward doors could be secured in such a way as to allow ordnancemen to use them as service platforms. (Author)

The inboard flap section of the Hellcat was an all metal structure while the outboard flaps were fabric covered. The Black area, outlined in Red, is a section of non-skid paint to give the pilot and crew better footing while boarding or working on the F6F (this is a non-standard addition, service F6Fs did not use non-skid). (Author)

There is a small triangular section between the inboard and outboard flap sections. There was no mechanical connection between the flap sections. Simultaneous operation of all flap sections was accomplished by the use of restrictor valves in the actuating cylinders. (Author)

The underside of the port flaps. The fabric covered outboard flap sections incorporated two inspection plates on either side of the lever arm attachments. Near the trailing edge of the outboard flap section are small drainage grommets. (Author)

Flap operation was hydraulic and electrically controlled. There was also an airspeed switch in the right stub wing section connected to the pitot-static system which would automatically retract the flaps at speed above 170 knots. (Author)

The rudder of a F6F-3 (BuNo 41930). The internally balanced rudder was a metal structure covered with fabric. The rudder trim tab was fully controllable via a trim wheel in the cockpit. The antenna post on the fin had a single wire that ran from this post to the antenna post mounted on the fuselage spine behind the cockpit. (Author)

The rudder trim tab was controlled via a trim wheel in the cockpit. The rectangular plate in front of the trim tab was the trim tab inspection plate. The circular rudder hinge inspection plate was located just under the White 5 on the fin. (Author)

The Erection and Maintenance Manual for the F6F-3 states that the apex of the star should be fifty-eight inches forward of the leading edge of the horizontal stabilizer, with the center ten inches below the leading edge. The star diameter is 50 inches and the Blue field is 56.25 inches in diameter. (Author)

The hole in the lower fuselage is the rear fuselage hoisting point. The hoisting sling was attached to a bar that was slid through the fuselage to lift the tail. (Author)

There are two push in doors on the fuselage for the pilot to use as hand and foot holds while boarding the aircraft. The White line was a guide for the pilot, if he ran his foot down along the line he would find the foot hold at the bottom. This line is over-sized, service F6Fs had a half inch White line and the push-in doors were Black. (Author)

The instrument panel of a F6F-3 (BuNo 04934). This was one of the first 200 Hellcats off the assembly line and does not have the gunsight installed. Several test instruments are in the cockpit, one directly under the panel, which appears to be an airspeed calibration instrument and a carburetor air temp gauge at the right. Flight instruments take up most of the primary panel with the exception of the RPM and Manifold Pressure gauges. Auxiliary instrument panel at the right contains the rest of the engine instruments. The magneto switch is on the far left side of the panel. The White placard on the left console is a schematic of the fuel system. (Grumman)

30

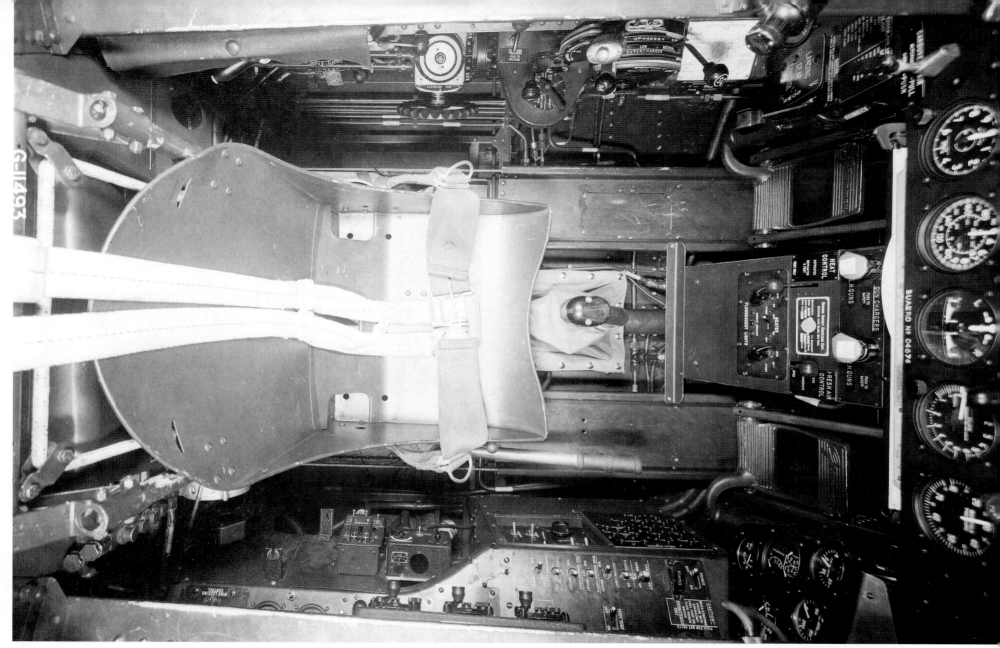

While the general cockpit layout of the F6F-3 was similar to the F4F Wildcat, it was much more complex. The Wildcat had mechanical linkages to operate aircraft systems, such as cowl flaps and landing gear, while the F6F had hydraulics. The hydraulic system operated the landing gear, flaps, gun charging, cowl, oil cooler, and intercooler flaps. The electrical system was also much more complex. The electrical system controls were located on the starboard console. Grimes florescent lights are located on the canopy sill and could be pointed where the pilot needed them. (Grumman)

The Hellcat had a retractable tie down hook under each wing. When not in use, the hook retracted up into the wing. The hook was released manually by a push on the fastener. (Author)

The windshield of a F6F-3 had a reinforcement brace running from the windscreen back to the rear frame. This restored F6F-3 is missing the armor glass normally mounted just behind the windshield. (Author)

There are two recognition/position lights on the fuselage spine of the F6F. The forward light was White and was deleted on the 1,298th F6F-5 and all later airframes. (Author)

This late style windshield is mounted on a F6F-3, which is highly unusual. Normally, the late style windshield was used on F6F-5s. One of the main visual differences was the deletion of the brace. (Author)

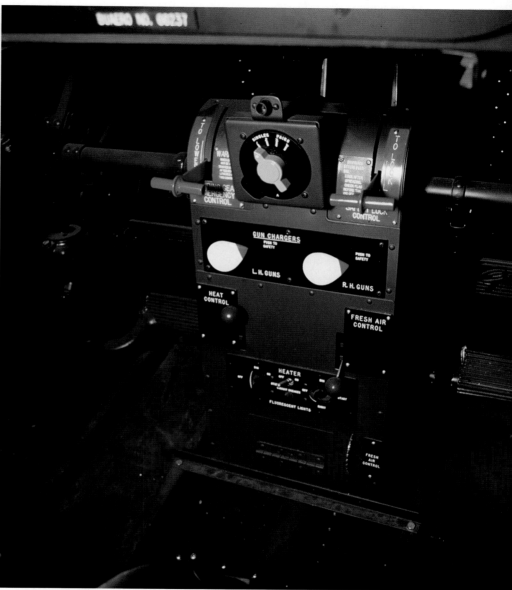

The electrical distribution panel was located on the right side of the cockpit. The row of clips that run vertically next to the seat are for pyrotechnic storage. The hydraulic hand pump is visible under the seat. The canopy crank handle is located at the upper left. (Lieutenant Ken Acosta)

The center console and rudder pedals of the National Museum of Naval Aviation's F6F-3. The two Red T handles at the top of the console are the landing gear emergency control (left) and the wing fold safety lock control (right). The two White knobs are the gun charging controls. Below them are the cabin heat and fresh air controls. (Lieutenant Ken Acosta)

The left console of F6F-3 (BuNo 04876). Visible are the landing gear retraction handle and indicator on the small auxiliary instrument panel along with a copy of the takeoff and landing check lists. The throttle quadrant contains the throttle, supercharger, mixture, and propeller pitch controls. Just below the throttle quadrant is the fuel selector control and other fuel system controls. To the rear of the throttle quadrant is the rudder/aileron/elevator trim controls. The tailwheel lock is on the rear deck of the console with the oil cooler and intercooler controls being located on the upper ledge just behind the throttle quadrant. (Grumman)

The starboard console of F6F-3 (BuNo 04876). The large handle near the bottom is the hydraulic hand pump. The circuit breaker panel is just above the pump handle and the gun control panel is to the right of the breaker panel. Main electrical distribution panel is forward on the console, with the recognition light panel, hydraulic pump selector valve, pressure gauge, landing gear emergency dump pressure gauge and wing lock control also located on this console. The large crank at the upper left is the canopy crank. Radio controls are located behind the canopy crank. Slight changes were made to this panel over the production life of the F6F-3, especially in armament controls and radio/IFF switching. (Grumman)

(Above) The Mk VIII gunsight on the National Museum of Naval Aviation F6F-3 (BuNo 66237) and a portion of the armored glass panel that is just forward of the gun sight. (Lieutenant Ken Acosta)

The instrument panel of the NMNA F6F-3. Flight instruments are all on the center panel while most of the engine instruments were located on a small panel to the right of the main panel. The landing gear handle is the White cube and the Red T handle is the alternate air door control for the auxiliary stage supercharger. (Lieutenant Ken Acosta)

The radio controls were all located on the right side of the cockpit. Below the radio cluster is the recognition light control panel and hydraulic hand pump. The pilot's hand held microphone is also visible in the center. (Lieutenant Ken Acosta)

The headrest and back armor plate on Pensacola's F6F-3 Hellcat. The headrest has a leather extension that snaps to the armor plate just behind the seat. It is obvious that the Hellcat had poor rearward vision, even with the small windows on the F6F-3. These windows were deleted on the later F6F-5. (Lieutenant Ken Acosta)

The seat and shoulder harness of the National Museum of Naval Aviation's F6F-3. The seat was painted in Interior Green while the rest of the cockpit was in Zinc Chromate Green. The pilot's seat pack parachute acted as a seat cushion. (Lieutenant Ken Acosta)

The windscreen of a F6F-3 (BuNo 08867) looking rearward through the gunsight. The pilot's armored headrest is visible as is the top of the antenna mast and a portion of the instrument panel coaming. This style of windshield, where the bullet-resistant glass was an integral part of the windshield was used on most late F6F-3s, F6F-3Ns and all F6F-5s. (Grumman)

The same F6F-3 looking forward through the windscreen. The gunsight has been removed revealing the Canon plug that supplied electrical power to the sight. Flight instruments are located on the left side of the panel and engine instruments are located on the right. As with any production aircraft, there were slight changes made to the instrument layout throughout the production life of the F6F. (Grumman)

The primary identification feature of the F6F-5 from the F6F-3 was the windshield and canopy. The windshield was made of flat armor glass and had the upper brace deleted. (Grumman)

The small rear window was deleted between the 1,500th and 2,000th F6F. Early F6F-5s retained the window, while all late production aircraft had it deleted. The pilot of this Hellcat has draped his earphones over the gunsight. (Tailhook)

Grumman F6F-5 Hellcat

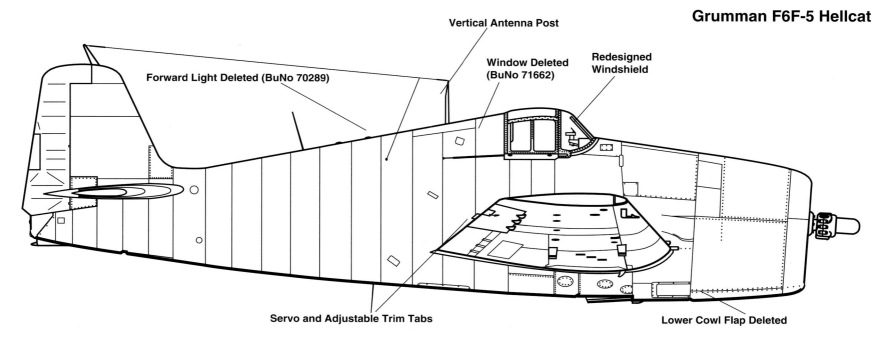

Vertical Antenna Post

Window Deleted (BuNo 71662)

Redesigned Windshield

Forward Light Deleted (BuNo 70289)

Servo and Adjustable Trim Tabs

Lower Cowl Flap Deleted

The seat, headrest and armor back on the New England Air Museum F6F-5. All Hellcats had armor plate behind the pilot's head, however, the armor was installed in at least two different positions. Some Hellcats had the armor flush with the cockpit bulkhead, while others had it canted forward, as this F6F-5 does. (Larry Webster)

The instrument panel and rudder pedals on the New England Air Museum's F6F-5. The cockpit interior is painted in Interior Green with a Flat Black instrument panel. This F6F-5 is the most accurate restoration in the world today. The Black panel under the instrument panel is the rocket selector panel. (Larry Webster)

The New England Air Museum's F6F-5 is not intended to fly again and has been restored to stock condition, without the need for modern avionics. The instrument panel of the F6F-5 featured a night illumination system that would illuminate the instruments in Red. The gunsight is a Mk VIII type. (Larry Webster)

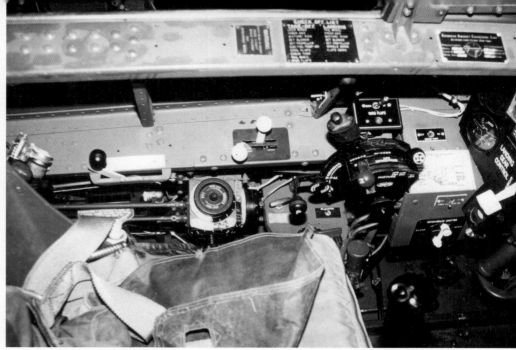

The left console of a F6F-5. There are a number of different Black and White placards on the Interior Green cockpit sill. The foremost plate is the Grumman factory plate that gave information such as aircraft BuNo and date of manufacture. (Larry Webster)

The right console of the F6F-5 is taken up with electrical and communications panels. This F6F has original IFF (Identification Friend or Foe) equipment. The round device near the center of the panel is the pilot's hand held microphone. (Larry Webster)

The windshield and gunsight of F6F-3 BuNo 41930. This aircraft has been modified with the later style windshield used on the F6F-3N, F6F-5 and F6F-5N. The aircraft is fitted with a Mk VIII gun sight (fully operational). The Red button on the side of the fuselage is the exterior canopy release. Service aircraft did not have this painted Red. (Author)

It took four and three quarter turns of the hand crank to open or close the canopy. The canopy was made of Plexiglas and was jettisonable. The side panels could be opened in an emergency. The canopy would also be locked at intermediate positions by the use of hand crank locking pins. (Author)

F6F-3

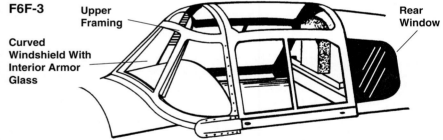

Upper Framing

Curved Windshield With Interior Armor Glass

Rear Window

F6F-3N/5/5N

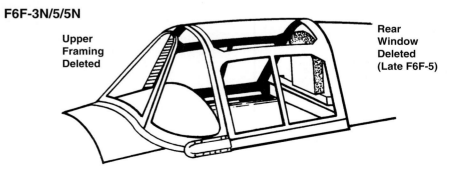

Upper Framing Deleted

Rear Window Deleted (Late F6F-5)

The canopy in the fully open position. The upper portion of the canopy was bulged upward to give the pilot more head room and was unframed for excellent upward view. The upper framing on the windscreen of the F6F-3 was deleted greatly improving forward view. The headrest in this Hellcat is made of Black leather and is attached directly to the rear bulkhead. (Author)

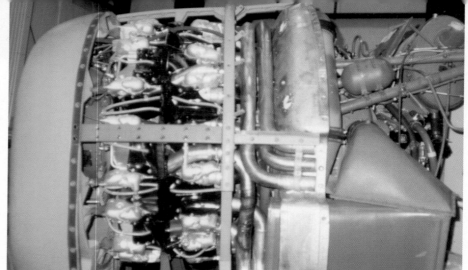

The Hellcat engine cowling consists of five pieces, two left, two right and an armored lower section attached to the frame with Dzus fasteners. The engine oil tank is visible at the top right. The small Green tank attached to the engine mount is the propeller oil pressure accumulator. (Larry Webster)

(Left) A Quick Engine Change (QEC) kit prior to installation on the New England Air Museum's F5F-5. The upper exhaust stacks are visible above the intercooler duct, with the lower exhausts exiting just below the duct. The interior colors are both Zinc Chromate Green and Interior Green (darker color). (Larry Webster)

A Pratt & Whitney R-2800-10W engine from a F6F-5 on an engine stand for restoration. The cylinders are Aluminum and the crankcase is Engine Gray. (Larry Webster)

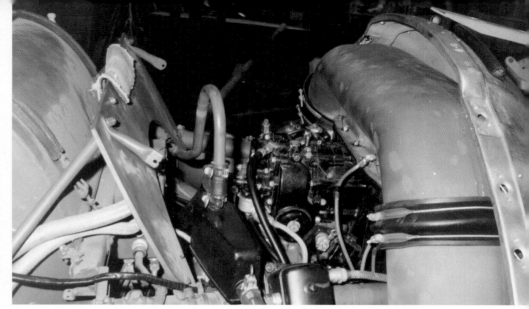

Combustion air entered the carburetor via ducts from the supercharger. Fluid lines were color coded. The Red-Black lines coming from the carburetor induction signify a vent tube from a closed compartment. The Light Blue-Yellow line is a purge line. (Larry Webster)

The forward crankcase houses both engine magnetos and the propeller governor. Immediately behind the magnetos is the ignition harness. The cowling has been primed with Zinc Chromate Yellow. (Larry Webster)

A Hellcat QEC kit waiting to be installed on a F6F-5. The engine accessory section, intercoolers and oil tank are all visible. Armor plate is installed in front of the oil tank. The carburator is located just behind the propeller pitch control accumulator (small Green tank). The oil tank held nineteen gallons. (Larry Webster)

The F6F-3N Hellcat night-fighter carried an AIA airborne intercept radar in a streamlined pod near the starboard wing tip. The pod had a diameter of twenty-four inches. It is believed that this aircraft is the XF6F-3N prototype during its testing at the Grumman facility. Eventually, 229 F6F-3Ns would be produced. Another radar equipped variant of the F6F-3 was produced, the F6F-3E, which carried the AN/APS-4 radar in a jettisonable pod under the wing. This aircraft was produced in much smaller numbers (eighteen) than the F6F-3N. (Grumman)

Radar Pods

F6F-3E   **F6F-3N/5N**

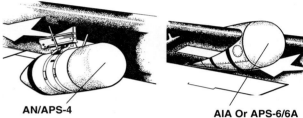

AN/APS-4   AIA Or APS-6/6A

The radar pod on the F6F-3N carried the AIA radar, while the identical pod on the F6F-5N carried either an APS-6 or APS-6A radar. (Grumman)

The radar jettison toggle switch is just above the throttle quadrant in the F6F-3E night fighter. The AN/APS-4 airborne intercept radar was carried in a pod under the starboard wing. Only eighteen F6F-3Es were built. (Grumman)

The starboard side console of a F6F-5N Hellcat night-fighter. The armament panel is located just to the rear of the circuit breaker panel. The pilot's hand held microphone rests in the center of the console. (Grumman)

The instrument panel of a F6F-5N Hellcat night-fighter. The airborne intercept radar scope was mounted in the center of the panel just below the gunsight. The F6F-5N was originally equipped with the Sperry AIA radar, but late production models had the AN/APS-6 or 6A radar. (Grumman)

The port console of a F6F-5. Over the course of production a number of minor changes were made to the console, including repositioning the intercooler shutter control to a position forward of the throttle quadrant. (Grumman)

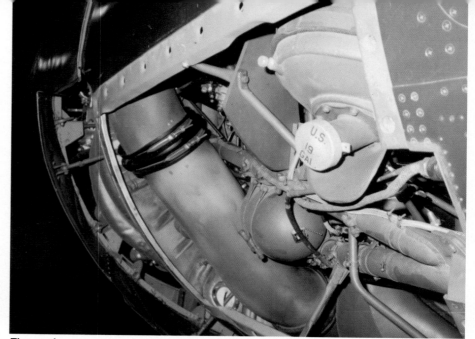

A built up engine assembly on a work stand prior to installation on F6F-5 BuNo 79192. The oil cooler is in place on the lower portion of the engine. Also visible are the cowl flap actuating rods, protruding from the heat shield. (Larry Webster)

The back side of the engine. The intake ducts are Gloss Black and the crankcase is Engine Gray. Red plastic dust covers have been placed in the exhaust ports. (Lieutenant Ken Acosta)

The engine accessory section and cowl flap actuators. As with most systems on the Hellcat, the cowl flaps were hydraulically opened and closed. The heat shield just behind the engine is visible, as is the oil tank armor plate. (Larry Webster)

The lower engine cowling section of BuNo 79192 has been removed to expose the lower port side of the Pratt & Whitney engine. The restoration team have used both Zinc Chromate Yellow and Zinc Chromate Green primers. (Larry Webster)

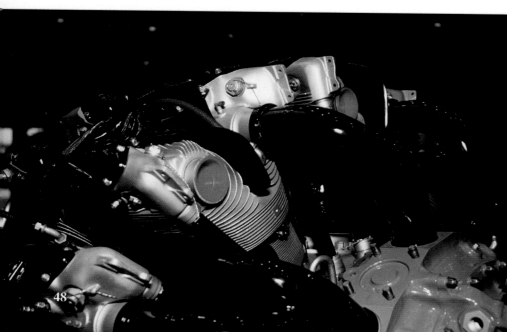

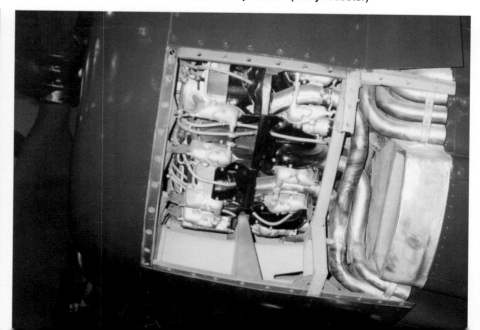

The Hellcat was powered by a Pratt & Whitney R-2800-10 series radial engine, generating some 2,000 horsepower. Starting with the 1,900th F6F-3 (BuNo 40634) all following Hellcats were fitted with the R-2800-10W with water/alcohol injection. These can be identified by the small access panel on the starboard fuselage just behind the cockpit. (Lieutenant Ken Acosta)

The propeller governor housing was located above the engine crankcase between the engine magnetos. (Lieutenant Ken Acosta)

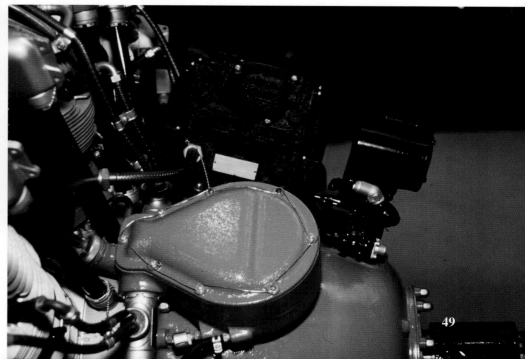

A Pratt & Whitney R-2800-10/10W radial engine on display at the National Museum of Naval Aviation reveals some details of the ignition harness. The cylinders are Natural Metal , as is the ignition harness. Spark plug wire flexible shielding is Copper. Also visible are the engine push rod tubes, which were painted Gloss Black. The engine crankcase was Engine Gray. (Lieutenant Ken Acosta)

The port bomb rack on a F6F-5 (BuNo 72223) loaded with a 250 pound M28 fragmentation cluster bomb. This Hellcat was involved in a series of ordnance tests to check bomb and catapult bridle clearance . (Grumman)

The starboard bomb rack on the same F6F-5 was loaded with a 500 pound M29 fragmentation cluster bomb. The sway braces on the front and rear of the bomb were used to keep it steady. The bomb rack used on the Hellcat was the Mark 51-7 and was capable of carrying bombs weighing up to 2,000 pounds. The bombs were electrically or manually released. (Grumman)

F6F Early Underwing Bomb Rack

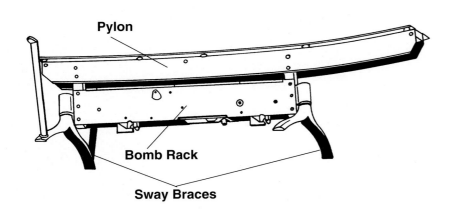

Pylon

Bomb Rack

Sway Braces

Standard F6F Underwing Bomb Rack

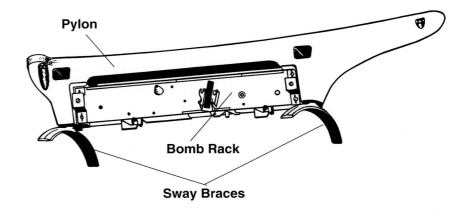

Pylon

Bomb Rack

Sway Braces

A late production F6F-3 in the landing configuration. The F6F-3 carried only one bomb rack, located on the starboard stub wing. The object hung on the bomb rack is a Mk 47 practice bomb dispenser . The oil cooler doors are in the open position. (Tailhook)

This F6F-3 has just taken the cut signal from the landing signal Officer (LSO). The empty single bomb rack used on the F6F-3 is visible under the starboard wing. (Tailhook)

(Right) A F6F-3 of Fighting One (VF-1) runs up prior to launch from USS YORKTOWN. The catapult bridle is not hooked up indicating this will be a deck run takeoff. The Flight Deck Officer is using hand signals to tell the pilot to run up the engine, when he is satisfied that all is ready, he will give the launch signal. The under fuselage fuel tank is secured in place by two safety bands, as well as two forward sway braces. (Tailhook)

The under fuselage fuel tank is secured in place by two safety bands, as well as two forward sway braces.

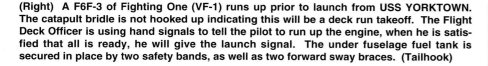

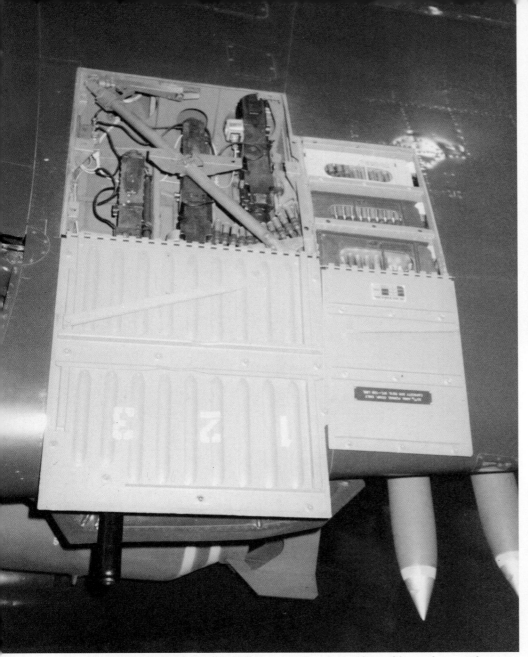

The Hellcat had provisions to carry the unguided 5 inch High Velocity Aircraft Rocket (HVAR). The rockets were first installed on the 3,451st F6F-3 (BuNo 42185) and all later production aircraft. There are metal blast covers on the flaps. (Larry Webster)

The Hellcat could carry a total of six 5 inch HVARs on Zero length launcher stubs. The rocket bodies are Light Gray, the nose is Olive Drab with a Yellow ring and a Silver tip. The rockets were usually fired in salvos of two each. (Larry Webster)

The New England Air Museum's F6F-5 was restored complete with gun bays and ammunition. Ammunition boxes were color coded according to size. The gun bay doors also acted as servicing platforms. This particular aircraft is equipped with the standard gun armament of six .50 caliber machine guns. (Larry Webster)

The port gun bay of a F6F-5. The guns are staggered withing the bay to ease ammunition feed problems. The Hellcat could carry a total of 2,400 rounds of .50 caliber ammunition. (Larry Webster)

The gun bay doors were hinged at the leading edge and could act as servicing platforms. The guns are numbered from port to starboard starting with the outboard gun on the left wing. The interior of the gun bay was Zinc Chromate. (Larry Webster)

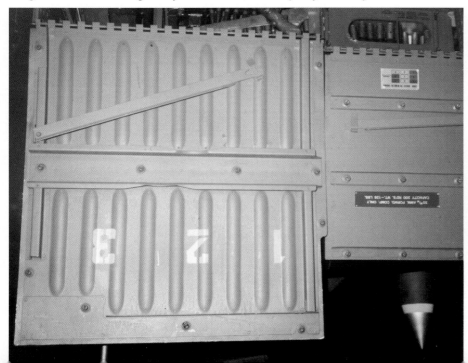

The Hellcat's primary armament consisted of guns, bombs and rockets. This Hellcat is armed with six .50 caliber machine guns, a 500 pound bomb and six 5 inch HVAR rockets. (Larry Webster)

53

5 Inch HVAR Rocket Installation

Grumman technicians install zero length rocket launcher stubs under the wing of a F6F-5 (BuNo 79675) on 21 February 1945. The opening above the technician in the foreground is an Amber/Green/Red light used by the LSO to determine if the aircraft was on the proper glide slope for landing. (Grumman)

This F6F-5 of VF-74 carries a 500 pound bomb on the wing bomb rack and empty rocket stubs. The name "Dorothy" was written on the bomb in chalk. The catapult hold back at the rear of the Hellcat is visible. (Tailhook)

Five inch High Velocity Aircraft Rockets on the zero length stubs under the wing of the New England Air Museum F6F-5 Hellcat. This was the standard air-to-ground rocket used by the Navy during the late war period. (Larry Webster)

This standard armament for most F6F variants was six .50 caliber Browning M2 heavy machine guns, three in each wing. These guns were the standard used on most Second World War American fighter aircraft. (Author)

The three guns were staggered with the outboard machine gun being recessed within the wing and the inboard gun extending far in front of the wing leading edge. All F6F-5s could replace two of the .50 caliber machine guns with a 20MM cannon for additional fire-power. (Grumman)

Gun Installations

Early F6F-3s

Faired Guns

Late F6F-3/F6F-5

Unfaired .50 Caliber Machine Guns

Alternate Gun Installation

.50 Caliber Machine Guns

20MM Cannon

The port gun bay of F6F-5 BuNo 72188. The diagonal reinforcement tube has been pivoted out of the way to provide access to the guns. The guns were electrically heated by elements located over the breech. This Hellcat carries a mix of four .50 caliber machine guns and a two 20MM cannon. Gun removal was made through an access hatch just forward of the wing flaps. (Grumman)

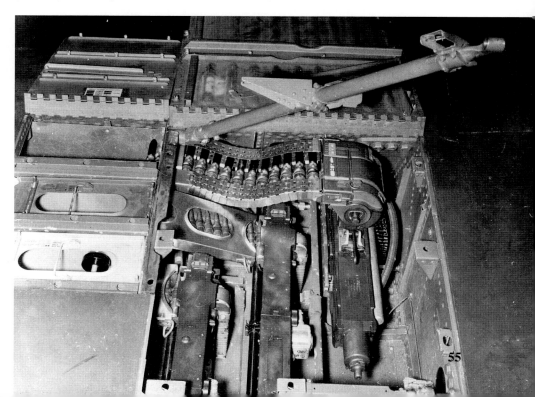

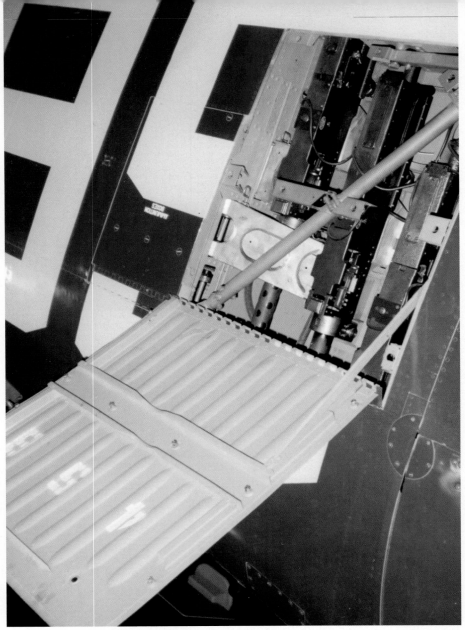

The starboard gun bay of the New England Museum's F6F-5. All the guns are in place, however, the ammunition chute for the inboard gun has been removed and the link ejector chutes have also been removed. The gun bay is painted in Zinc Chromate. The gun bay door is hinged on the leading edge and held in place with Dzus fasteners in the closed position. (Larry Webster)

Guns four, five and six are installed in the starboard wing. The ammunition access panels are closed. The diagonal brace in the gun bay is removable, to provide more accessibility to the guns. (Larry Webster)

A 500 pound general purpose bomb (complete with nose fuse) hung on the bomb rack of a F6F-5. There is a small access panel forward of the bomb rack for access to the gun camera. (Larry Webster)

Just to the rear of the centerline fuel tank was the target towing attachment fitting. This was used to allow the Hellcat to tow a gunnery sleeve target for squadron practice aerial gunnery. (Larry Webster)

The starboard bomb rack on F6F-5 (BuNo 93879) owned and operated by the Planes of Fame Air Museum in Chino, California. This aircraft was a very late production F6F-5 and had bomb racks attached to both stub wings. The paint scheme carried by the aircraft is inaccurate (it carries an F6F-3 three tone scheme), since late F6F-5s were all delivered in overall Gloss Sea Blue. It was not unusual to see a F6F-3 in the overall Gloss Sea Blue scheme, since they were often repainted after major overhauls. (Author)

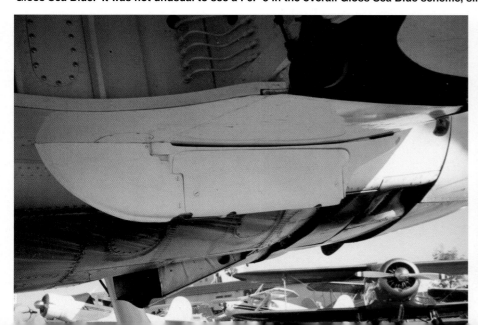

Grumman build eighteen F6F-3E, all delivered during January of 1944. The F6F-3E carried a Westinghouse AN/APS-4 radar in an antenna mounted under the starboard wing. The pod could be jettisoned in an emergency. (Grumman)

Standard bomb racks on a F6F-5 fitted with a Mk 47 practice bomb dispenser. The bomb dispenser is Light Gray. This dispenser could carry eight Mk 4 Practice bombs internally. The Mk 47 was the Navy's standard bomb dispenser and could be carried by most Second World War Navy aircraft. (Larry Webster)

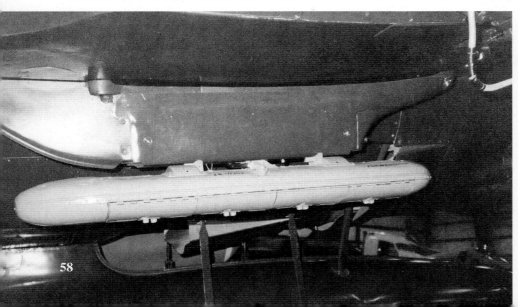

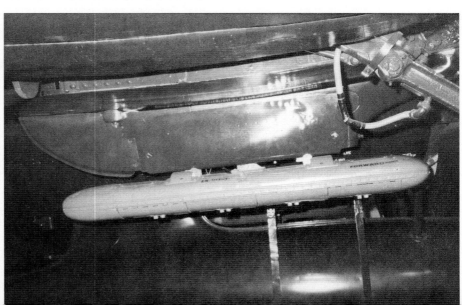

The Hellcat carried a number of different style drop tanks on the fuselage underside, although each was the same capacity, 150 gallons. Both of these Hellcats are carrying different tanks. The aircraft in the background has a White early style 150 gallon tank with a curved mounting pylon and vertical seams. The Hellcat in the foreground carries the late war style 150 gallon tank with a straight mounting pylon and horizontal seam. Both aircraft use stabilizing bands and sway braces to keep the tanks in place. (Richard Hargis)

A pair of VCN-2 F6F-5N Hellcats await their launch from an unidentified carrier. The front of the AN/APS-6 radar was painted White. The aircraft in the foreground was armed with the alternate gun armament of two 20мм cannon and four .50 caliber machine guns. The pitot tubes of these aircraft are Gloss Red, the standard delivery color. The main landing gear doors and door attachment brackets are in Insignia White. (Tailhook)

Three F6F-5Ns of VCN-2 based at NAS Key West, Florida. They carry an unusual mix of markings. The two aircraft in the foreground have small national insignia, while the aircraft in the background has the standard large insignia. The wing marking on the aircraft in the background wraps over the radar pod. The main landing gear doors are painted Insignia White. All three aircraft carry the alternate gun armament of four .50 caliber machine guns and two 20ᴍᴍ cannons. F6F-5Ns flew alongside F4U nightfighters in Navy composite squadrons , however, the Corsair was to remain in service longer, seeing action in the Korean War.

This is a late war modified Mk 12 under fuselage 150 gallon drop tank. This tank has the seam running horizontal and a straight pylon. (Larry Webster)

The spike in the center of the circular inspection plate fits into a recepticale on the 150 gallon drop tank. (Grumman)

The underside of the Hellcat fuselage with the skinning removed reveals the centerline drop tanks racks and plumbing. The object at the top is the oil cooler. (Larry Webster)

This is the final style under fuselage tank carried by the F6F. The Mk 12 tank was also carried by the F7F Tigercat and F8F Bearcat. This tank was retained by the Navy into the 1970s. This tank did not use a solid attachment pylon. (Tailhook)

This overall Gloss Sea Blue F6F-5 Hellcat of Fighting Forty (VF-40) clearly shows the normal wear patterns on the gloss paint. There are c0rdite streaks on the wings from firing the six .50 caliber machine guns, which seem to disappear near the ammunition access bays. The upper engine exhaust pattern stains the fuselage and extends down onto the upper wing surface near the wing root. (Tailhook)

A Hellcat pilot outfitted for high altitude flight during 1943. He has an oxygen mask, leather helmet and late style goggles. Cloth helmets were also common, especially in the more humid climate of the South Pacific. (Tailhook)

Lieutenant Junior Grade Eugene R. Hanks of VF-16 in the cockpit of his F6F-3 aboard USS LEXINGTON (CV-16) during 1943. He was an ace with five kills, all in one day. This F6F-3 had the early style windshield with the armor glass panel internal to the windscreen. Heated air was circulated between the two panels, which caused dust to become trapped, reducing forward visibility. (Tailhook)

A line-up of F6F-3Ks with lengthened tail wheel struts. Because of this modification, the tail wheels were fixed in the down position. Tail colors denoted the assigned radio frequency of the drone. (Tailhook)

(Right) The antenna on the fin of the F6F-3K was unique, The two extra antenna wires running down from the bar on the antenna post to the fuselage were for the remote control equipment in the drone. (Tailhook)

An overall Insignia Red F6F-3K with a Yellow Orange tail section. Hellcats such as these took part in Operation CROSSROADS, one of the atomic bomb tests. The aircraft carried special instruments through the nuclear cloud and other dangerous tasks. (Tailhook)

This F6F-5N (BuNo 72827) was assigned to Marine Nightfighting Squadron 533, VMF (N)-533 on le Shima on 27 June 1945. The aircraft carried the name LITTLE NANCE on the nose in White. The squadron codes on the fuselage were in Black . (Rowland P. Gill via Tailhook)

The Royal Navy received a total of 252 Hellcat Mk I (F6F-3). These aircraft saw service in both Europe and the Pacific. (Grumman)

The XF6F-6 was an attempt to boost the performance of the Hellcat. There were two prototypes built (BuNos 70188 and 70193) and these were powered by 2,100 hp Pratt & Whitney R-2800-18W air-cooled radial engines driving four blade propellers. This was the same engine that powered the F4U Corsair and since all available engines were needed for Corsair production, the XF6F-6 did not enter production. Top speed for the prototypes was 417 mph. (Grumman)

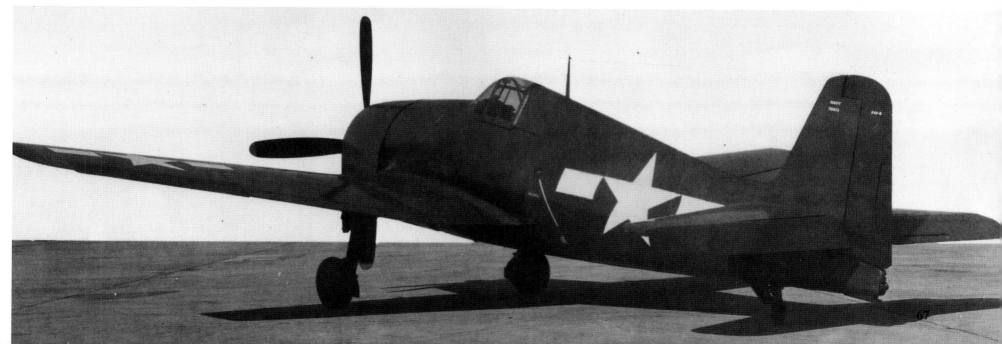

An early F6F-3 of Fighting Four (VF-4) flies over the California countryside. The aircraft is Blue Gray over Light Gray with the national insignia in six positions. The aircraft number appears on the nose, fuselage side and on the top of the wing. The gun port fairings were discontinued with the 910th production F6F-3. (John Fry)

Two F6F-3 Hellcats on a factory test flight prior to installation of their gun sights and other final equipment. The national insignia has a Red surround, indicating that these aircraft were delivered sometime during the Sumer of 1943. (John Fry)

This colorful F6F-3 Hellcat was used as a drone controller aircraft at Naval Air Station Johnsville, Pennsylvania. Controller aircraft would fly formation with the drones, using electronic remote control to fly them. The controller aircraft were always given a highly visible color scheme. (Tailhook)

Several Hellcats were transferred to the National Advisory Committee on Aeronautics (NACA) for use as variable stability research platforms. Modifications to this Hellcat include the installation of a data probe on the port wing, and two probes on the starboard wing. The rudder trim tab was also enlarged. NACA operated this aircraft into the 1960s. (Tailhook)

This F6F-3 was used to test the field of fire for the gun turret on the Lockheed PV-2. The aircraft was painted overall Glossy Sea Blue, highly unusual for an F6F-3. The propeller hub was in White. (Carman deAmico via A.C. Brooks)

A Royal Navy Hellcat Mk I (FN322) in the Dark Slate Gray/Dark Sea Gray over Sky camouflage scheme. The Royal Navy received a total of 252 Hellcat Mk Is (equal to the F6F-3) originally naming the aircraft the Gannet. This was quickly changed to avoid confusion with the American navy. (Mark Aldrich)

The XF6F-2 was another experimental prototype built from F6F-3 (BuNo 66244) The aircraft was powered by a Pratt & Whitney XF-2800-16 turbosupercharged engine with a redesigned cowling. The aircraft was named "FUZZY WUZZY" because of the yarn tufts applied for filming. (Grumman)

This aircraft (BuNo 02981) started life as the second Hellcat built. It was fitted with a R-2800-10 engine becoming the XF6F-3. It also served as the prototype for the XF6F-4 with a R-2800-27 engine. It also served as a test bed for an all cannon armament. It was finally scrapped in October of 1946. (Grumman)

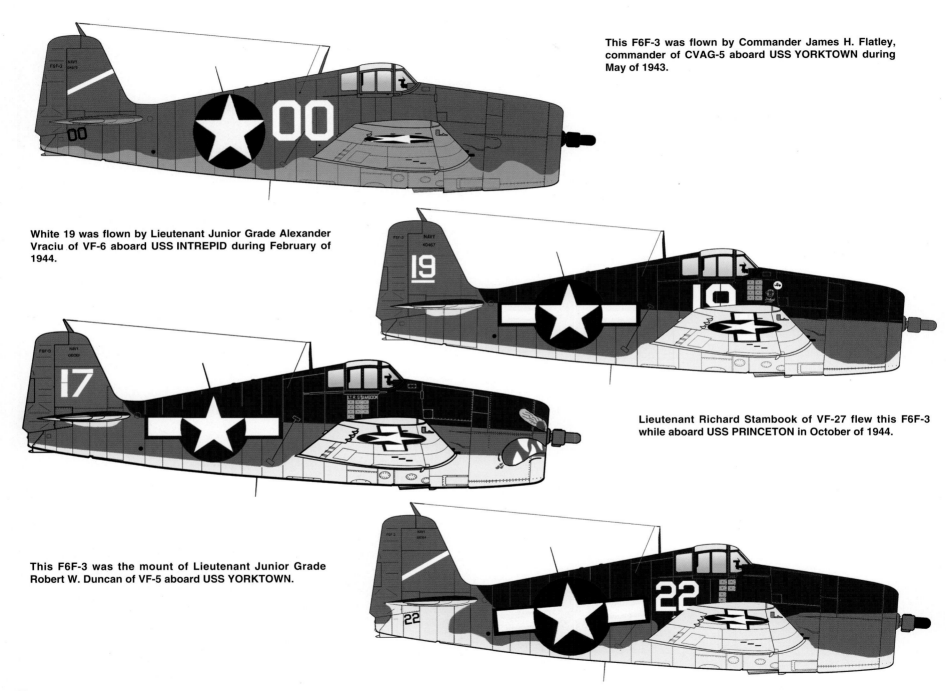

This F6F-3 was flown by Commander James H. Flatley, commander of CVAG-5 aboard USS YORKTOWN during May of 1943.

White 19 was flown by Lieutenant Junior Grade Alexander Vraciu of VF-6 aboard USS INTREPID during February of 1944.

Lieutenant Richard Stambook of VF-27 flew this F6F-3 while aboard USS PRINCETON in October of 1944.

This F6F-3 was the mount of Lieutenant Junior Grade Robert W. Duncan of VF-5 aboard USS YORKTOWN.

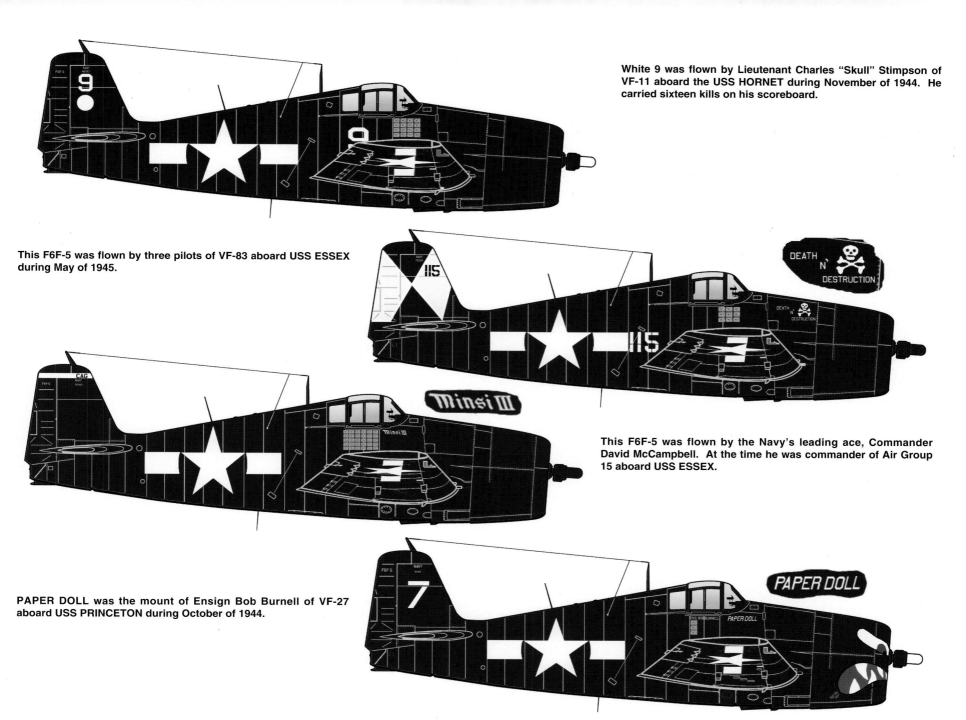

White 9 was flown by Lieutenant Charles "Skull" Stimpson of VF-11 aboard the USS HORNET during November of 1944. He carried sixteen kills on his scoreboard.

This F6F-5 was flown by three pilots of VF-83 aboard USS ESSEX during May of 1945.

This F6F-5 was flown by the Navy's leading ace, Commander David McCampbell. At the time he was commander of Air Group 15 aboard USS ESSEX.

PAPER DOLL was the mount of Ensign Bob Burnell of VF-27 aboard USS PRINCETON during October of 1944.

A pilot starts up the engine of a F6F-3K drone. The aircraft was overall Insignia Red with a Black anti-glare panel. A number of surplus to requirements F6Fs were converted to drones for use as aerial targets. Some were outfitted with wing tip flare pods and were used during the early testing of the AIM-9 Sidewinder air-to-air missile. Hellcats converted to drones were overhauled and converted at NAS Pensacola, Florida. (Tailhook)

A F6F-5K drone is readied for launch during 1952. This drone is carrying a 1,000 pound bomb on the centerline rack to attack targets in Korea. Six drone F6Fs were used as make-shift guided missiles to attack targets such as railroad tunnels and other highly defended targets. (Tailhook)

A line-up of F6F-3K drones sometime prior to 1947 (old style national insignia). These aircraft were overall Insignia Red with various colored tails. They were used for a number of missions including taking air samples during some of the atomic tests, where a human pilot would have been in extreme danger. (Tailhook)

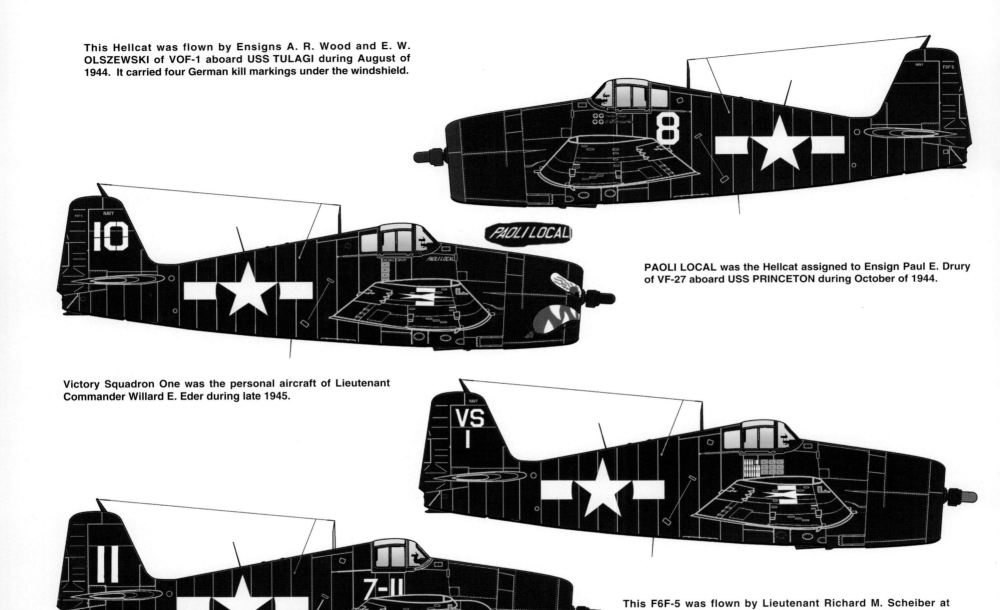

This Hellcat was flown by Ensigns A. R. Wood and E. W. OLSZEWSKI of VOF-1 aboard USS TULAGI during August of 1944. It carried four German kill markings under the windshield.

PAOLI LOCAL was the Hellcat assigned to Ensign Paul E. Drury of VF-27 aboard USS PRINCETON during October of 1944.

Victory Squadron One was the personal aircraft of Lieutenant Commander Willard E. Eder during late 1945.

This F6F-5 was flown by Lieutenant Richard M. Scheiber at NAAS Charlestown, SC during August of 1945. It still carried its factory delivery number, 899, on the nose.

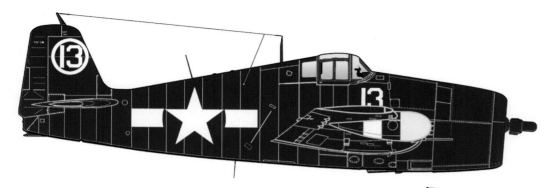

White 13 was flown by Lieutenant William E. Henry of VF(N)-41 aboard USS INDEPENDENCE during September of 1944.

Black Death was the personal mount of Major R. Bruce Porter, commander of VMF(N)-533 on Okinawa during June of 1945.

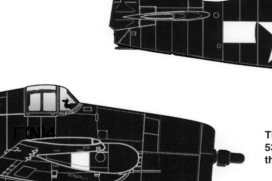

This F6F-5N was assigned to Captain Robert Baird of VMF(N)-533 during June of 1945. The aircraft code F(N)4 was carried on the fuselage in Black.

Lieutenant Commander Stanley G. Orr of No 804 Squadron, Fleet Air Arm flew this Hellcat I while aboard HMS EMPEROR during 1944.

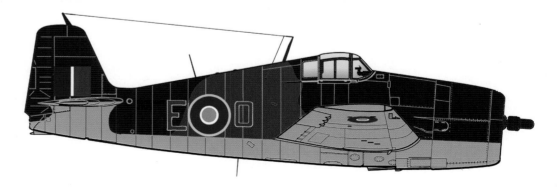

A pair of F6F-5s of the reserve squadron based at NAS New York (Floyd Bennett Field) fly in formation on a training mission. They carry the star and bar insignia that came into use during 1947. Both aircraft appear to have had their International Orange reserve bands painted out with Gloss Sea Blue and both are fitted with zero length rocket stubs. (Sid Bradd)

Following the Second World War, the F6F Hellcat was, for the most part, withdrawn from active service. Some F6F-5Ns remained in fleet service in composite squadrons as all-weather/night-fighters until 1954. Reserve units also flew the Hellcat in the fighter-trainer role, although it did not have a lengthy career in reserve squadrons. The last Hellcats, remote control drones, were phased out in May of 1961. This F6F-5 (BuNo 79603) was assigned to Naval Air Station New York (Floyd Bennett Field). It carries the International Orange band around the rear fuselage identifying the aircraft as being assigned to the reserves. The reserve band had a width equal to that of the outside diameter of the fuselage national insignia Blue roundel. All numbers were in White. (Sid Bradd)

A Royal Navy Hellcat II of No 889 Squadron during 1945. At this time Hellcats were being delivered to the Fleet Air Arm in the standard U.S. Navy overall Gloss Sea Blue scheme.

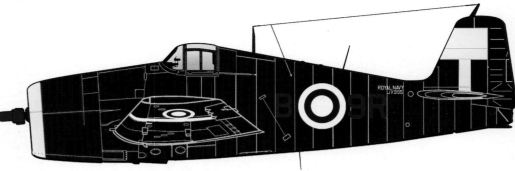

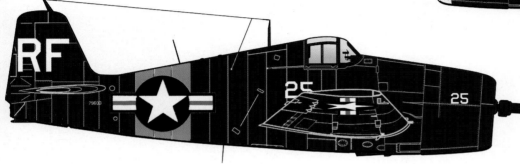

A F6F-5 of the Naval Reserve out of Naval Air Station New York (Floyd Bennett Field) during 1947.

This French Navy F6F-5 saw combat in the air-to-ground role over Vietnam during the first Indochina War.

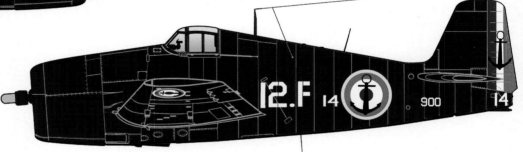

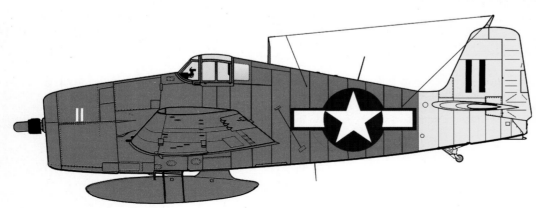

A F6F-3K drone based at Naval Air Station Atlantic City, New Jersey during March of 1946. These drones were later used in Operation CROSSROADS, one of the atomic bomb tests.